THE ART
OF
WOOD BURNING

THE ART OF WOOD BURNING

by
Connie Krochmal
and Karen Snipes

745.51

DRAKE PUBLISHERS INC.
NEW YORK, NEW YORK 10016

Published in 1974 by
Drake Publishers Inc.
381 Park Ave. South
New York, N.Y. 10016

Copyright © 1974 by Connie Krochmal and Karen Snipes.
All rights reserved.

Library of Congress Cataloging in Publication Data

Krochmal, Connie and Karen Snipes
    The art of wood burning.

  1. Pyrography.   I. Title.
TT199.8.K76   745.51   74-6132
ISBN 0-87749-675-7

Printed in the United States of America.

Contents

Chapter 1. History and Wood Burning 3

Chapter 2. Tools, Equipment, and Supplies 13

Chapter 3. The Raw Material—Wood 27

Chapter 4. Template Making 67

Chapter 5. Projects 73

Chapter 6. Finishes 89

Acknowledgments

A number of people have generously helped us to prepare this book.

Dr. Dick Thomas of the School of Forestry, North Carolina State University provided us with a number of wood samples for trial burning, and advised us on the chapter on wood structure as well as providing us with photos of wood structure.

Dr. Nanette Henderson enlisted her 13 year old sister, Kim Marie Smith, Baltimore, and Ann DeLon Riggan, Warrenton, North Carolina, a high school student, to do the sketches in the back of the book, and the samples of wood burning we have included.

Our good friends the George Hoadleys of Raleigh, North Carolina lent us their Zulu reverse wood burning; and the Arnold Droozs of Cary, North Carolina lent their Soviet wood-burned salt cellar, and Barbara Davey of Raleigh the lovely wood tray she made in high school.

Lasercraft, Optical Engineering, Inc. of Santa Rosa, California, sent samples of their new craft of laser burning.

Stephen Hanover, Extension Forest Resources, North Carolina State University and Harry Leslie, Public Information Specialist, Forest Products Laboratory, Forest Service, U. S. Department of Agriculture, Madison Wisconsin provided the color photos of different woods. Charles Balducci of Raleigh assisted with some of the photography.

As always, Dr. I. T. Littleton, Director, D. H. Hill Library, North Carolina State University and his wonderful staff provided the help possible to make this book a success.

THE ART
OF
WOOD BURNING

CHAPTER 1

History and Wood Burning

Man's discovery of fire as a tool in its own right has been the keystone of his advance towards a civilized society.

The first major use of fire was for cooking, which ultimately freed our primitive ancestors from the compelling necessity to hunt every day. Cooking of food made it possible to keep foods in an edible condition for longer periods of time. All of this took place about 100,000 years ago. To this day, in the Stanley Owen Mountain of Papua, New Guinea, all of the community pigs are slaughtered at one time, and then cooked over a fire. The meat is then preserved, to be used later over a period of time. This is a remnant of a very, very old and honored tradition.

About 70,000 to 80,000 years ago the use of fire to harden wooden hunting spears became part of man's collection of skills. As time passed, the utilitarian use of fire to fashion weapons was broadened to include other techniques as well, including designs and ornamentation.

Man also found he could use fire to make a basic means of transport for rivers and oceans; the canoe. By using the giant trees of the forest, and fire to make these trees into hollow pointed vessels, he soon found his life enriched by being able to wander further away from the home fire to see new sights and observe people of nearby tribes.

With more "free" time and a fuller stomach, art began to become a part of primitive man's life. Whether paintings daubed on walls of caves, or intricately burned designs on wood, man's cultural climb once started, never has stopped.

One of the fascinating Indian activities that caught the attention of the early settlers was the method used to make canoes (Figure 1). Probably the first report was written by the Englishman, Thomas Harriot in the late 1500's, who commented:

> The manner of making their boats in Virginia is very wonderful. For wheras they want Instruments of iron, or other like ours, yet they know how to make them handsomely, to sail on their rivers, and to fish with all, as ours. First they choose some long thick tree, according to its diameter, and make a fire with dried moss of trees, and chips of wood so that the flame should not mount up too high and burn too much of the length of the tree. When it is almost burnt through, and ready to fall they make a new fire, which they suffer to burn until the tree falls of its own accord. Then burning of the top and branches of the tree in such a way that the body of the tree may retain its full length, they raise it upon poles which are forked posts, at such a reasonable height as they may handsomely work upon it. Then they take the bark with certain shells. They reserve the innermost part of the length for the nethermost part of the boat. On the other side they make a fire according to the length of the body of the tree, sawing at both the ends. Then when they think it is sufficiently burned they quench and scrape away with shells, and making a new fire they burn it again and so they continue sometimes burning and sometimes scrapping until the boat has sufficient reason to make things necessary to serve their needs."

To this day, in remote parts of the world, in parts of South America, and in Papua, New Guinea, wood burning is a much used tool of creativity and art, flourishing where Western civilization rarely penetrates.

In Papua, canoes used in fishing as well as for travelling along the coast and up the dark inland rivers, are still hewn and burned as they were once made in the United States (Figure 2). The huge garamat drums used for village ceremonials and to send messages in Papua are still made and crafted with fire (Figure 3).

In Colombia, South America, very intricate, wood burning patterns of Mayan origin are made in the villages and make

ART OF WOOD BURNING 5

Figure 1. "The manner of makinge their boates." This beautiful sketch comes from the 1893 edition of Harriot's *Narrative of the First English Plantation of Virginia*. From an engraving by Theodore dy Bry based on a drawing made by John White, made about 1585. *Duke University Library.*

their way to the markets. Because they require a good deal of labor, they are becoming very difficult to find. Two of the items we have shown (Cover photo and Figure 4) were lent to us by Howard Harper Jr., who has lived in Colombia for many years.

A very unusual technique was brought to our attention, while we worked on this book, by Dr. George Hoadley of North Carolina State University.

In Zululand in South Africa, Dr. Hoadley found unusual and handsome examples of "reverse" wood burning technique (Figure 5).

With this method, slabs of wood an inch or two in thickness are placed over a fire and allowed to char, but not burn too deeply. The design is then made by scraping around a sketch or design, with the image remaining black and the surroundings rubbed away to the original wood color. This is an attractive

Figure 2. Canoes made by fire are still very much in use in parts of the world. Here is one on the Sepik River of Papua. Department of Information and Extension Services, Government of Papua, New Guinea, Port Moresby.

ART OF WOOD BURNING

technique and one that the home craftsman can use if he or she has access to either an indoor or outdoor fireplace. One of the harder woods would be easier to work with as burning can be controlled with less attention.

The newest method of wood burning really calls for the latest 20th century technological know-how.

A laser beam, a beam of pure light, is focused on a very minute spot thus raising the temperature of the wood and causing vaporization of the area of focus. The depth of the burning is controlled by the length of time the spot is exposed as well as the strength of the laser.

Figure 3. The large and thrilling garamut drums are used to send messages and carry rhythm for ceremonies. Built with fire burning this old and handsome drum still sounds the call in Aibom Village, East Sepik District, Papua. Department of Information and Extension Services, Government of Papua, New Guinea, Port Moresby.

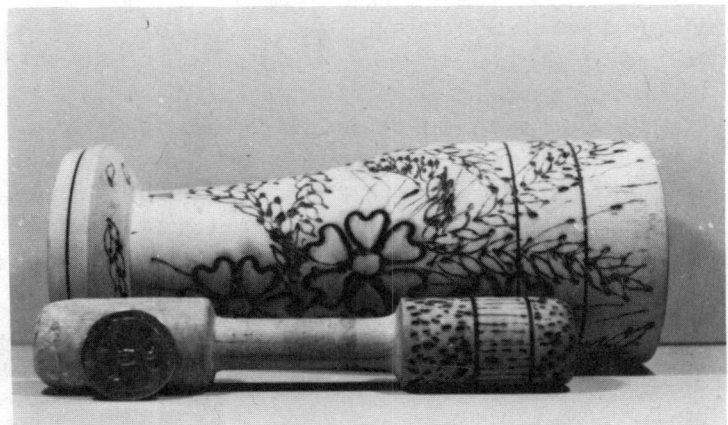

Figure 4. A wood burned mortar and pestle from the neighborhood of Bogota, Colombia. Dr. Arnold Krochmal.

Figure 5. "Reverse" burning as an art form in Zululand is different and most attractive. These African animals are vividly done with this technique. Charles Balducci.

10   ART OF WOOD BURNING

Very clean burning is achieved by this process even though there is no physical contact with the wood and the beam. An artist prepares a sketch which is used to control the beam so that it strikes only the areas intended for removal. This technique produces a three dimensional effect (Figure 6).

This is obviously not a method that lends itself to the home craftsman, but is of interest because of the beautiful work that is possible, and is indicative of the renewed interest in wood burning as an art form of unlimited potential.

Wood burning is even used in the Soviet Union as shown on this salt cellar (Figure 7).

In this modern age, there is a renewed interest in arts and crafts. Wood burning is one of the most respected and venerable of these crafts.

A beginning can be made with an electric pen and small pieces of wood. As a "feeling" develops for working with woods, more challenging opportunities present themselves. The use of the torch to shape as well as decorate wood is an opportunity for craft fulfillment of the highest order.

In the next chapter, we will learn something of the tools and equipment easily accessible to the home craftsman.

Figure 7. This wood-burned salt cellar is from the Soviet Union.

Figure 6. The unbelieveable cleanness and detail of this plaque were due to the careful use of the Laser Beam by a talented craftsman. Dr. Arnold Krochmal.

CHAPTER 2

Tools, Equipment, and Supplies

To progress with your newly discovered craft, you will need some tools and equipment which serve specific purposes. These tools can be bought as the need for them arise. There is no need to "stock up."

Electric pen

The most frequently used tool, the electric pen (Figure 8) and its overpoints, may be found in hobby shops and department stores. The pen itself is of standard size, though the overpoints are interchangeable and come in various sizes. The size of the overpoint would depend on the type of project.

To operate your electric pen, just plug it into a 100 volt outlet and allow it to heat for several minutes. Avoid touching the brass tip or ceramic tip with the hands and fingers. These parts become very hot and may cause painful burns if they are mishandled. To prevent accidents, lay the pen on its side so it will not touch anything when you are not using it.

Test the speed at which the pen is burning and the different curves and angles you can draw, on the back or bottom of the object to be burned or on a scrap piece of wood of the same kind you will use. If after some use the point should become dirty, clean it off gently with a piece of very fine sand paper.

Use a pointed overpoint or sharp edge to outline the picture by slowly moving the pen toward you. By straightening or leaning your pen in the direction of motion you will find it easier to move sideways and around curves and corners. Move only as fast as the tip will burn. The depth and width of the burned design are related to the pressure exerted on the pen, the speed at which you are moving the pen, and whether the pen is straight up or down at a slant.

After you have finished outlining the design, you may wish to bring out the background areas. For a solid background use the flat face of the wide line overpoint, again moving only as fast as the pen can achieve the desired darkness. For a more textured appearance use short quick strokes to achieve the effect you want (Figure 9).

The electric pen usually comes with a set of overpoints to fit over the original tip to create varied effects. The overpoints make the kind of lines they do because their shape controls the amount of heat passing through them, and delivers the heat to certain areas. There are usually six overpoints included with the pen (Figure 10). They are:

1. the pencil tip for shading and curves
2. the wide line tip for foil and shading
3. the narrow line tip for foil and shading
4. a foil writing tip
5. a leather and cork tip
6. a tip for foil writing on plastics

The *pencil point* is good for dots and foil writing but is not good for lines or curves because it doesn't glide easily or smoothly, but instead burns little dots which makes the line look uneven. Pencil and needle point are equally suitable for foil writing.

Figure 8. This is the electric pen, the basic tool needed in beginning wood burning. The original point is at the left, in the ceramic base.

ART OF WOOD BURNING   15

Figure 9. This lovely wood burning of an evergreen tree and its cones was done on a scrap piece of wood, using the narrow line overpoint.

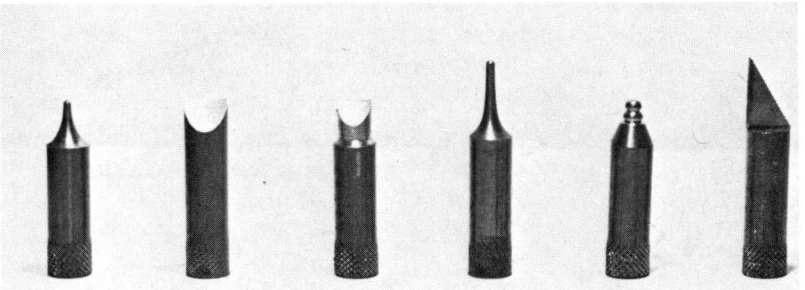

Figure 10. These are the 6 available overpoints.
   1. for curves and shading
   2. wide line for foil and shading
   3. narrow line for foil and shading
   4. writing on foil
   5. cork and small dots
   6. narrow lines

The *chisel point* or *wide line* is for pressing short strokes. It can not be easily moved if pressed directly on the end of the round point but it makes a very fine even line if you turn it on its side. Makes corners and curves very well, as well as a ¼-inch wide burned hole or circle.

The *narrow line point* is for foil writing and shading.

The *foil writing tip* or *needle point* is for very fine lines, dots, and curves, and leather. Very even movement is required because leaving in one place for very long causes it to burn tiny dots which makes the burning uneven, unless of course, if the dots are to be part of the pattern. It makes a wide shallow burned line.

The *leather* and *cork tip,* or *round point* is similar to the chisel point in use.

The tip for *foil writing on plastics* has a lower temperature and does not burn as quickly. It makes a very thin line. It does not do well turning curves and is not suitable for use on wood surfaces.

Other overpoints that may sometimes be available with kits include the screw point, the hole cutting point and the blade point.

The *screw point* is useful for burning circular patterns dots.

The *hole cutting point* was designed for burning holes in leather, but can also be used to burn large deep circles in wood by placing the point down, burning for the allowed time, and removing to the next spot that is to be burned.

The *blade point* is like the original electric pen in design. Because the temperature is lower, it does not burn as quickly as the electric pen without a point. It cannot be turned on its side for shading. Use only the front blunt part because the back part drags and causes uneven burning. The very front of the tip can also be used to burn holes or dots rather than changing to the special hole point. This tip does not do well burning curves. For an interesting pattern, try putting the whole point down and you will have a wedge shaped line. It makes a wide line for foil burning.

ART OF WOOD BURNING   17

With practice and experience you will learn the capabilities and limitations of each overpoint.

Alcohol and propane torches

The next important piece of equipment you will buy, will be an alcohol or a propane torch. Each torch has a limit to its capabilities. The direction you want to take with your wood burning will determine the torch you will need (Figure 11).

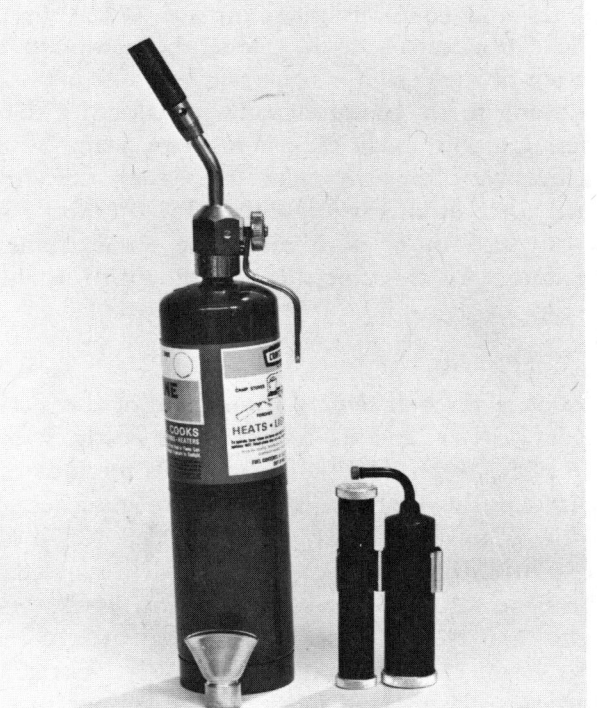

Figure 11. The small alcohol torch which uses denatured alcohol is shown on the right.

The large butane torch to the left, is over twice as big. In front of the butane torch is the spreader which permits burning over a wider area.

Alcohol torch

The alcohol torch is small; only 6 inches high, light, and inexpensive to operate. Its fuel is denatured alcohol; easily purchasable at drug stores. This torch is best suited for fine and intricate work. The alcohol torch can easily burn the wood around the edges of the template* without damage to the template or the wood beneath because the flame is not as hot as that of the propane torch. Since the temperature is not as high, the templates do not buckle and warp where there are sharp curves and edges in the template. When warping does occur, the flame can "crawl" under the template and burn the wood out of the design.

The alcohol torch has disadvantages along with its many advantages. Caution must be taken when using it. Improper handling or overfilling can cause it to catch fire. In addition, holding the torch at an angle less than 15-20° from a horizontal position can also cause it to catch fire. Be extremely careful when working with this torch as you should be when working with any type of flame.

Propane torch

The propane torch is quite the opposite of the alcohol torch. It is larger, heavier, and its fuel is more costly. It is approximately 18 inches high. The flame from this torch covers a much wider area than the alcohol torch. The propane torch, unlike the alcohol torch, can be held at any angle. When the flame spreader is attached the area covered is nearly doubled.

The propane torch is best used to hollow blocks of wood for large bowls and trays, for sculpturing logs and blocks, and to burn large designs into blocks of wood. As mentioned before, the propane gas burns at a much higher temperature than the alcohol. This may cause the templates to warp when heated with a propane torch for too long. You can alleviate some of the warping of templates by heating slowly and evenly over the entire surface moving the torch continuously. The propane torch will often warp a template with sharp curves or points

---

*A template is a piece of shaped metal placed over the wood to prevent your burning into the design. More on templates later.

ART OF WOOD BURNING

in a design. The flame may then crawl under the template and ruin the pattern.

The disadvantages of the propane torch is its bulkiness. If you bring the torch too close to the wood it causes the flame to go out.

Asbestos glove

This is needed to protect your hand from the torch heat when moving and handling the hot templates. No ordinary kind of glove will do because you need the fireproofing qualities of asbestos (Figure 12).

Asbestos pad

It is needed to protect the surface you will do your burning on. A pad 12" x 12" will do nicely for a beginner. Any other material besides asbestos will not protect the work surface (Figure 12).

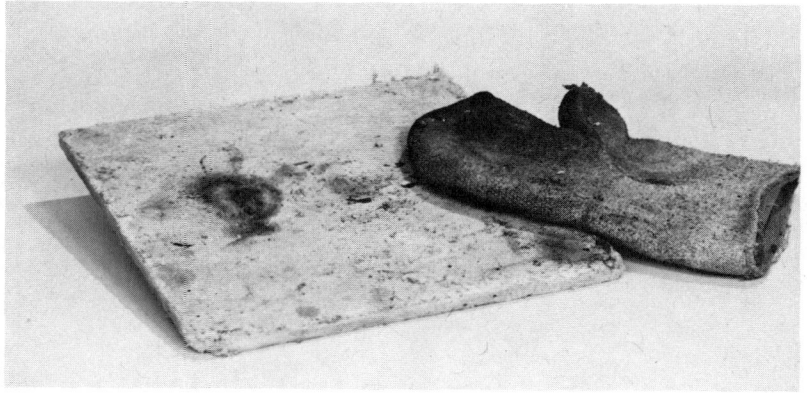

Figure 12. Our much used and highly valued asbestos glove is always on hand for "hot" work.

Equally indispensable for smaller work is the asbestos pad, another basic safety device.

Ball peen hammer

You need a hammer with a metal face to pound your templates flat. We prefer a 6-ounce model. Rubber or rawhide mallets are not efficient since they will not pound out the rough edges of the templates. You will find many varied uses for a hammer during your work (Figure 13).

Cold chisel

These types of chisels are made specifically to cut through metal. They can be used to cut metal in places where your tin snips will not reach. Choose the size you find most easy to work with. We prefer a ⅜ inch model for both convenience and accuracy (Figure 13).

Jewelers saw

No other saw can achieve the fineness of detail you may need. You can cut smooth curves in sheet metal when making

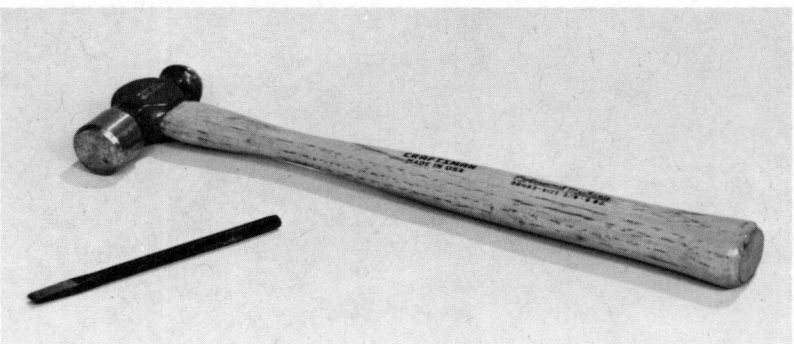

Figure 13. Our six ounce ball peen hammer is relatively lightweight, but strong enough to serve our needs in template making.

We find this ⅜-inch cold chisel most comfortable to use in cutting templates, particularly those with curves.

ART OF WOOD BURNING

templates without producing jagged edges. It is important to keep the blade rigid and tight in the frame with the blade teeth pointing towards the handle. Hold your metal securely so that it doesn't slide and cause the blade to break (Figure 14).

Scribe or scratch awl

This tool is used to mark the lines of your template pattern onto the sheet metal. Pencil marks do not work well because they can be rubbed off and are hard to see. Use the scribe to mark the pattern onto the metal (Figure 14).

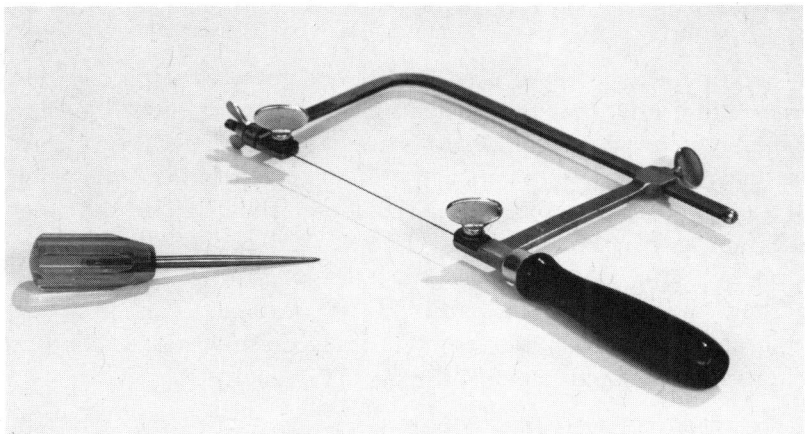

Figure 14. When you buy a jewelers saw, be sure to get at least twelve extra blades, as they do break. The scratch awl is available at hardware stores.

Spark lighter

The spark lighter takes the place of matches. It is much safer to use than matches because it keeps your hands away from the torch burner when trying to light the flame (Figure 15).

Steel wool

Ordinary steel wool will smooth your projects without ruining the texture and appearance of the burned surface. Size 000 is very fine steel wool and is recommended for finishing the project (Figure 16).

Sand paper

Sand paper should be used sparingly. Heavy sanding can ruin the texture and appearance of your project. Use only fine sand paper when you sand. Sand paper comes listed as coarse, medium or fine. If numbers are present on the back of the sheet of sand paper, remember that the larger the number the finer the sand paper. For example, no. 600 sand paper is much finer than no. 220. The four basic varieties of sand paper are flint, garnet, aluminum oxide and silicon carbide. The first are natural and the last two are synthetic, or man-made. For our purposes, flint sand paper is the best (Figure 16).

Steel brush

A steel brush is necessary to brush the burned wood out of trays and sculptures. Only use a brush with steel bristles. Other bristles may melt or disintegrate when used to brush out hot burned wood (Figure 16).

Tin snips

Ordinary scissors or cutters will be inadequate for our purpose. Tin snips are made specifically to cut metal. Pick a pair that are comfortable for your use. Tin snips are used to cut your

ART OF WOOD BURNING 23

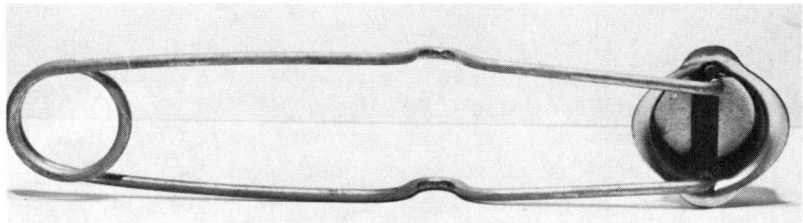

Figure 15. The spark lighter provides protection when lighting the butane torch. New flints are easy to install.

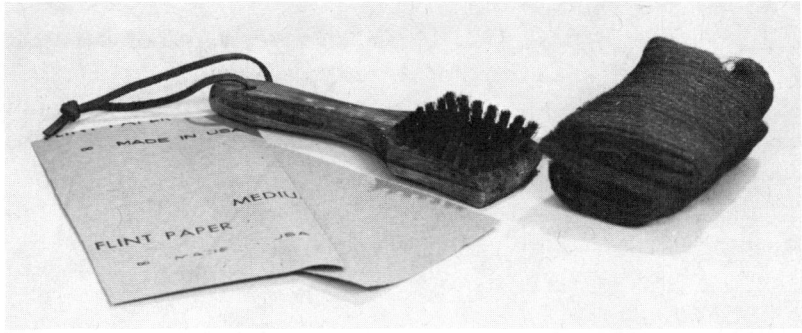

Figure 16. Standard large rolls of steel wool make a smooth finish an easy job. To avoid getting pieces of the wool in our hands we use it with work gloves.

We generally use medium and fine flint sand paper, although other types do just as well. Only use a steel brush to prevent burning of brushes made of other materials.

sheet metal for making templates. They cannot cut stainless steel (Figure 17).

Sheet metal

Sheet metal should be used for all your templates. Do not use galvanized sheet metal because it is zinc coated and hard to work with. Eighteen gauge sheet metal is easy to work with. Thicker metal can be used but is also more difficult to cut through.

SAFETY

We cannot emphasize too strongly the need for caution and safety in wood burning.
1. Two items we find indispensable are an asbestos glove and an asbestos pad (Figure 12). Both are available at biological supply houses and hobby shops. The pad is excellent to use while torching materials. With the gloves we change the overpoints even when they are hot, and can hold a heated template in position if needed (See dust jacket).
2. Remember that the electric pen does get very hot. NEVER try to change an overpoint barehanded while the ceramic heating element is hot. We use two pens, so that we do not have to wait too long to continue, and can alternate pens while one is cooling.
3. Always lay the electric pen on its side to keep the tip from causing damage or fire. If practical, lay it on the asbestos pad.
4. Be sure to disconnect the electric pen when you have finished with it.
5. When lighting the torch be sure the flame is facing a clear area. Check to be sure it is not turned toward you, a wall, or any wooden object. *Turn it off when not in use.*
6. In using the alcohol torch do not tilt it so far that the alcohol runs out. This can cause a fire.
7. Use a pair of work gloves while making templates and while using steel wool, as a protection against cuts and scratches.

ART OF WOOD BURNING 25

8. Be sure to use the spark lighter to light your propane torch. This keeps your fingers and hands away and out of the flame. Only use the matches to light the wick for the alcohol torch. If your wood catches fire smother the flame with the asbestos glove or pad. Do not allow it to keep burning as it would become hard to extinguish.

9. Burn small pieces of wood over your asbestos pad. Place larger pieces of wood on a non-flammable surface such as concrete, because your asbestos pad will not be big enough to protect the entire area.

10. Be sure to brush away from you when brushing out burned wood, to prevent sparks from setting your clothes on fire.

11. Do not wear clothes that will get in your way or that are so loose they may impede motion or catch fire.

12. For beginners, a handy tube of first aid cream might serve a real purpose!

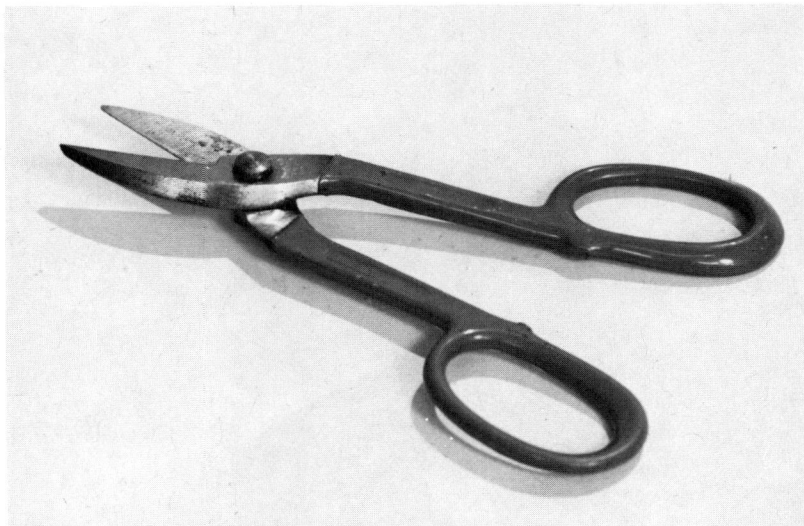

Figure 17. We use this small pair of tin snips because they are easy to handle. They can only cut the length of the blades, and then the cutting must be continued with the cold chisel or jewelers saw.

CHAPTER 3

The Raw Material—Wood

The purpose of this chapter is to explain why woods reveal different figure or grain patterns, and to provide information we have assembled for a variety of woods in our workshop. We will consider the burning adaptability of a number of woods. Knowledge of the relationship between wood structure and grain patterns will help you to select the proper wood to obtain desired grain patterns, as part of the wood burning art.

Wood grain basically is the difference between the "springwood" and "summerwood" found is every tree. The springwood is more porous than the summerwood. During spring the tree absorbs large quantities of water and grows at a fast rate. During the summer, growth is slower due to the relative scarcity of water. This accounts for the denseness or heaviness of the summerwood, compared to the porousness or lightness of the springwood (Figure 18). Often the springwood is lighter in color than the summerwood and this color difference is part of the wood grain. The rings produced during a year are the growth rings, often referred to as annual rings (Figure 19).

Trees are classified into two groups, softwoods and hardwoods. Most of the softwoods are evergreen trees, while the majority of hardwoods are *deciduous trees,* which shed their leaves. The softwoods, like some pines, are light and porous and usually easier to work with. Hardwoods like oak and walnut are dense and require more work. Burning rate varies with wood density. Lighter woods char more quickly than dense wood as you will see when comparing the rate of charring of springwood and summerwood. Springwood burns quickly, forming depressed, pithy areas; summerwood burns slower leaving ridges. This is referred to in wood burning as *ridging*.

In some species, the difference between springwood and summerwood is very gradual and fewer summerwood cells are produced. When this occurs, it is difficult to distinguish growth rings (Figure 20). Such woods are valued for carvings, as they possess more uniform density, easier to work.

The results obtained by burning and brushing wood depend largely on the species used. For those woods with extreme differences in the density of springwood and summerwood, distinct figures can be obtained. Woods which lack a sharp demarcation between springwood and summerwood have indistinct figures and unclear grains. The figures which show on the surface of wood are due to the exposure of the growth rings and their width.

Figure 18. This sketch shows why springwood (left) is more porous and less dense than summerwood (right). The springwood cells are large and thin walled. Summerwood cells (right) are smaller, more compact and denser. (Alan Lenk).

Figure 19. This photograph shows clearly the concentric rings of annual growth. The light colored zones are springwood and the dark colored zones are summerwood. (Maurice Krochmal).

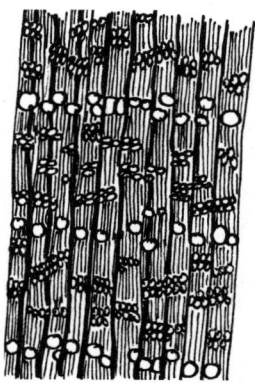 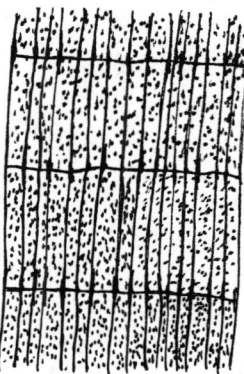

Figure 20. This sketch shows the difference between a wood with clearly visible annual rings (left) and wood in which essentially the same size cells are found and annual rings difficult to see. (Alan Lenk).

To summarize, woods with clear visible differences between springwood and summerwood are those which show distinct grain patterns.

We have provided two simple tables to help you select a wood for a specific creative purpose, as well as a more detailed, illustrated summary of wood qualities of interest to the craftsman.

Table 1. Some woods will provide distinct and obvious figures after burning and brushing. These are woods with markedly different springwood and summerwood.

Softwoods

hard pines
   pitch, yellow, longleaf,
   shortleaf, loblolly, Virginia
   and others

Douglas fir

larch

Hardwoods

oak

elm

ash

Table 2. More uniform texture and figure is generally provided by the following species because the difference between summerwood and springwood is not marked.

Softwoods

soft pines
   white, pinyon, and others

cedar

spruce

Hardwoods

basswood

yellow poplar

sweet gum

birch

In the following pages we have summarized the burning qualities of woods, as well as other qualities of importance to the wood burner. We will discuss these woods in alphabetical order. Here are some definitions of terms used in describing woods.

Grain. The arrangement and appearance of the components or parts that make up wood.

Interlocked grain. Wood in which growth is in one direction in a number of growth rings and then in an opposite direction in following growth rings, and then reverses again.

Pithy. A term used to describe a wood surface that develops numerous small holes, or spaces, visible to the eye, after flame is applied and the surface brushed. This is a practical definition and not meant for botanical use.

Ridging. The effect of burning springwood and summerwood grains produces depressed pithy areas alternating with lighter, more solid, less burned areas or ridges. The relative size of the pithy and ridged areas will vary greatly.

Shock resistance. It refers to the ability of a wood to withstand impact with another surface without splitting or cracking.

COMMON WOODS FOR USE IN WOOD BURNING

AMERICAN ELM   (Figure 21)

The American elm ranges in color from brown to dark brown and sometimes contains shades of red. It has a straight, and sometimes interlocked grain. It is a tough wood and rates high in shock resistance. American elm ranks moderately in hardness and heaviness. It is difficult to work with and has a low resistance to decay.

It is dense and after burning, you will notice that it does not char uniformly. Ridging occurs and long narrow slits develop in areas which char more heavily. Heavily burned areas are not parallel but follow the contour of the wood grain. After brushing, the heavily charred areas show a coarse pithy texture. The original color returns to the sunken areas giving an interesting color contrast between the burned wood and the original wood.

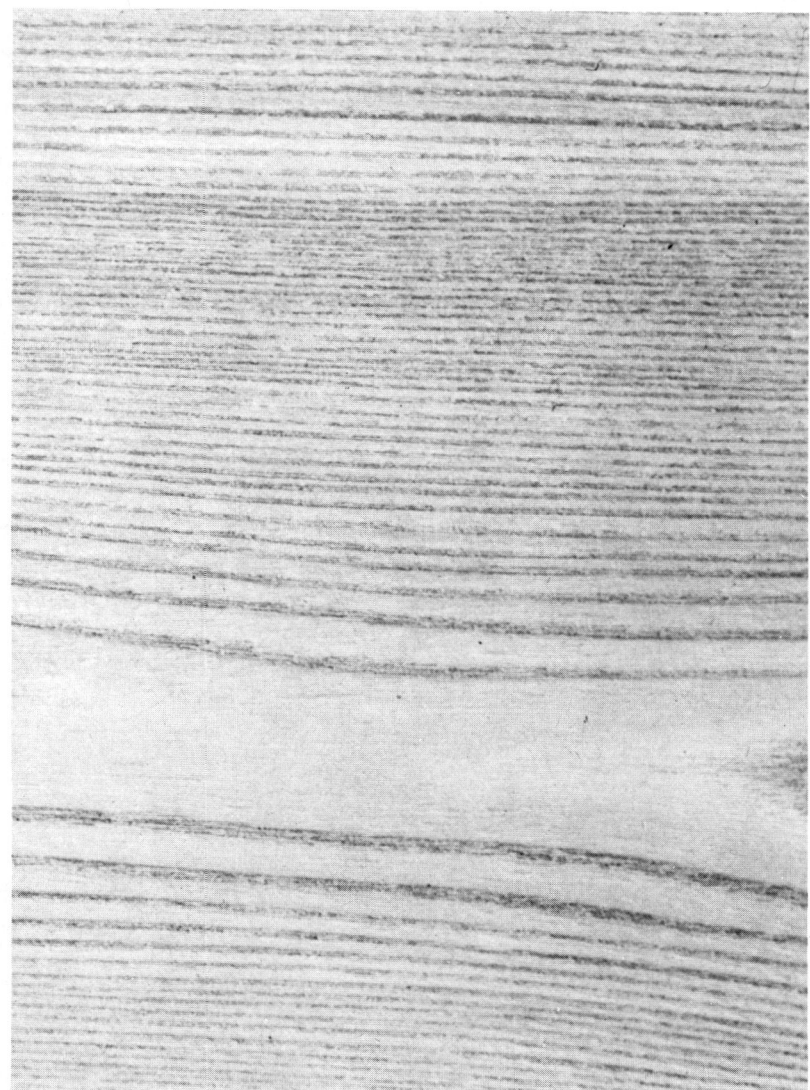

Figure 21. American elm

BASSWOOD   (Figure 22)

Basswood is a lightweight hardwood. It is moderately stiff and low in shock resistance. It is characterized as a weak wood. It is easy to work with hand tools and machinery tools. Basswood makes a fine smooth surface with a minimum of polishing.

Basswood burns easily and uniformly. No noticeable ridges form after burning and brushing. It forms a very smooth surface after brushing and using steel wool. Smooth brown color over a finely textured surface is characteristic of basswood.

Many of the craft shop items sold for burning are made of basswood. This is a recommended "beginners" wood.

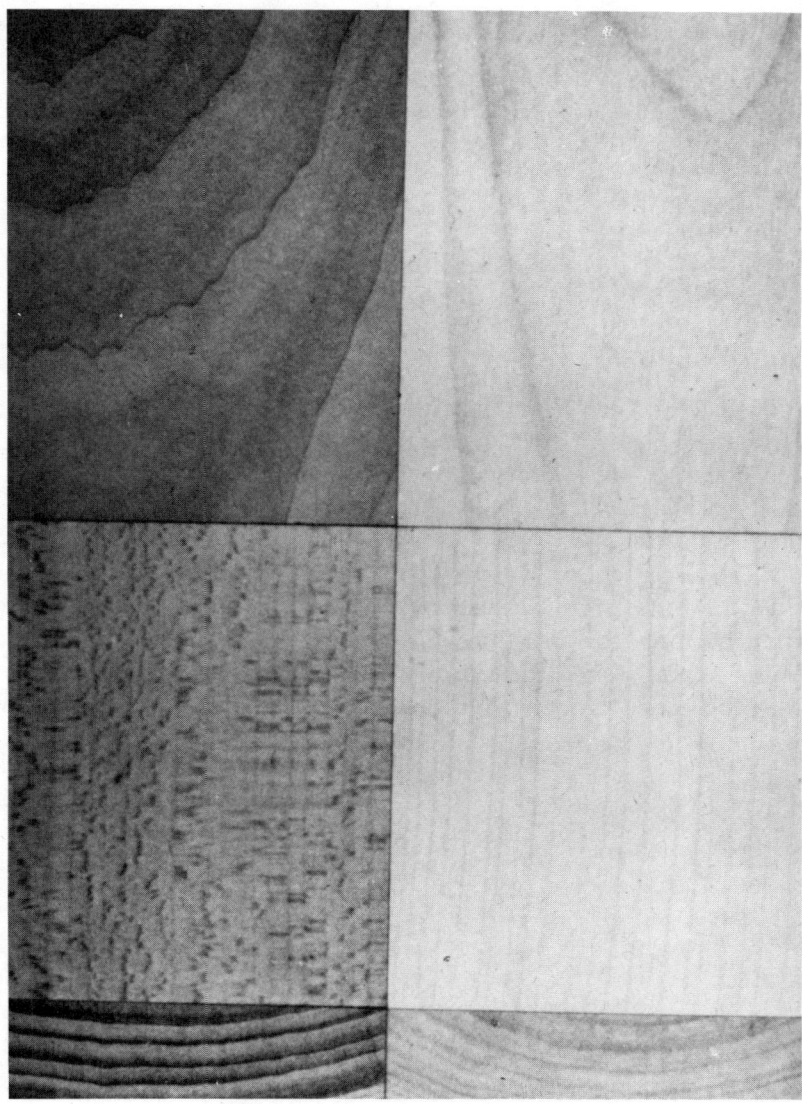

Figure 22. basswood

BIRCH (Figure 23)

Birch is a very heavy wood, light reddish brown in color. It ranks very high in shock resistance. The grain is not pronounced and does not show up well. It is difficult to work with because of its hardness. It takes on a very smooth lustrous finish with much polishing.

Birch is a dense wood with a close tight grain. It burns smoothly and evenly. Close observation will reveal tiny holes after burning and brushing. These small holes form an interesting texture over the entire surface. A smooth brown color over the entire surface is typical of burned birch.

Figure 23. birch

BUTTERNUT (Figure 24)

Butternut ranges in color from a light chestnut brown to a light grayish brown. It is a straight grained wood, and moderately soft. It is very lustrous and can be finished to resemble black walnut. It takes strain well and is quite high in shock resistance.

Butternut is not as dense as other hardwoods and burns easily. It produces an even surface after being burned. After brushing, ridging occurs. This wood has a small, uniform grain. It requires very little steel wool to finish smoothing the surface. This is another good wood for beginners to work with.

Figure 24. butternut

CHERRY   (Figure 25)

Cherry is very distinctive because of its coloring and smell. It is easily worked with both hand tools and machine tools. Cherry is usually straight grained and produces a handsome lustrous finish of reddish coloring. It is moderately heavy, stiff and responds well to shock.

Cherry is dense and therefore, is difficult to burn and requires a large amount of time to produce a finished piece. It has a very smooth surface after being burned. After brushing with a steel brush the surface remains smooth. Careful observation will reveal small darkened grain lines. However grain is not a pronounced feature in cherry as it is in some other woods. Burned cherry remains well darkened with none of the original wood color returning.

Figure 25. cherry

DOUGLAS FIR (Figure 26

This is a moderately heavy stiff and strong wood, moderately resistant to shock and easily worked with both hand and machine tools. Springwood and summerwood show little difference in color.

Douglas fir develops high distinctive ridges after being burned and brushed (See Figure 39). At the bottom of the ridge, the wood remains heavily burned while at the top of the ridge you will find that very little wood has been burned away. The top of the ridges burn dark brown while the base of the ridges burn light brown. These ridges run parallel over the entire wood surface. Small white slits appear in the surface after burning and brushing. A very pleasing color contrast can be obtained using fir, due to this formation of ridges during the burning process.

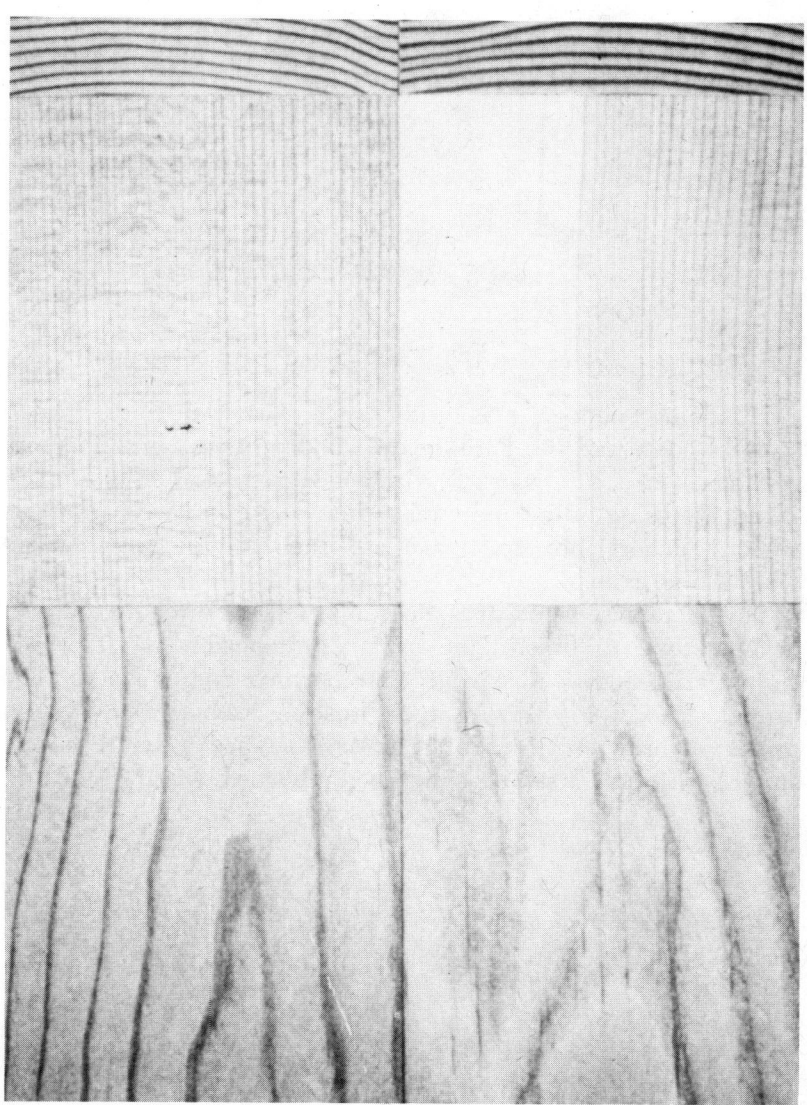

Figure 26. Douglas fir

HONDURAS MAHOGANY (Figure 27)

Honduras mahogany is generally a dark red color with a straight grain, and is a hard, heavy wood. It is very high in shock resistance. It can be worked with machine tools but is difficult if you are using only hand tools. Mahogany burns well and stays smooth under abrasion, makes a fine smooth surface, and takes a high polish.

This is a dense wood. It is difficult to burn and requires a great deal of time to finish. The grain of mahogany is small and closely knit, and is noticeable after burning and brushing. The original wood color remains after brushing leaving your finished project a brownish red color. Mahogany has a hard durable surface with only a small portion being burned out.

Figure 27. Honduras mahogany

MAPLE   (Figure 28)

Maple is generally a light reddish brown with straight grain. It is very hard and heavy and is very high in shock resistance. Maple is easily worked with hand tools and machine tools. It turns well, stays smooth under rubbing, makes a fine smooth surface, and takes a high polish.

It is difficult to burn and when burned, ridging occurs. Brushing the pithy depressions highlights the original color. The flowing grain pattern of maple can provide many interesting effects, combined with the solid smooth surface. Maple remains very dark after being brushed and regains most of its original color except at the bottom of the pithy areas.

ART OF WOOD BURNING 47

Figure 28. hard maple

RED GUM   (Figure 29)

Red gum, sometimes called hazelwood, ranges in color from a flesh colored gray to varying shades of reddish brown with darker grades often streaked. It has a handsome interlocked grain and is moderately hard and heavy. Red gum ranks high in shock resistance. It is easily worked with hand tools and machine tools.

Red gum is not as dense as other hardwoods. It burns easily and produces a smooth even surface. After burning, there is little evidence of any grain pattern difference. After brushing, the surface remains smooth in appearance and to the touch. The final product is dark in color.

Figure 29. red gum

RED OAK   (Figure 30)

Red oak is a very heavy wood and highly resistant to shock. It is a straight grained wood, usually grayish brown with a reddish tint, easily worked with most hand and machine tools, and produces a very lustrous smooth finish.

It is hard to burn because of its density. The grain pattern is very large and pronounced. When burned, ridging occurs. The original wood color can be seen in the bottom of the pithy sections of the grain area. With red oak, a wide variety of interesting grain effects can be attained.

Figure 30. red oak

SHORTLEAF PINE   (Figure 31)

Shortleaf pine is a moderately heavy wood, but is superior to the lightest of the Southern pines. It is moderately stiff and strong and moderately shock resistant. Like most southern pines, it produces a resin. It is easily worked with hand and machine tools and makes a fine smooth surface with little polishing.

During initial burning, the resin comes to the surface. After steel brushing, parallel ridges form, with the top being darker than the bottom. The tops of the ridge are medium brown shading to lighter brown at the base of the ridge. Resin slits are present before burning, but these slits are deeper and much more elongated after burning.

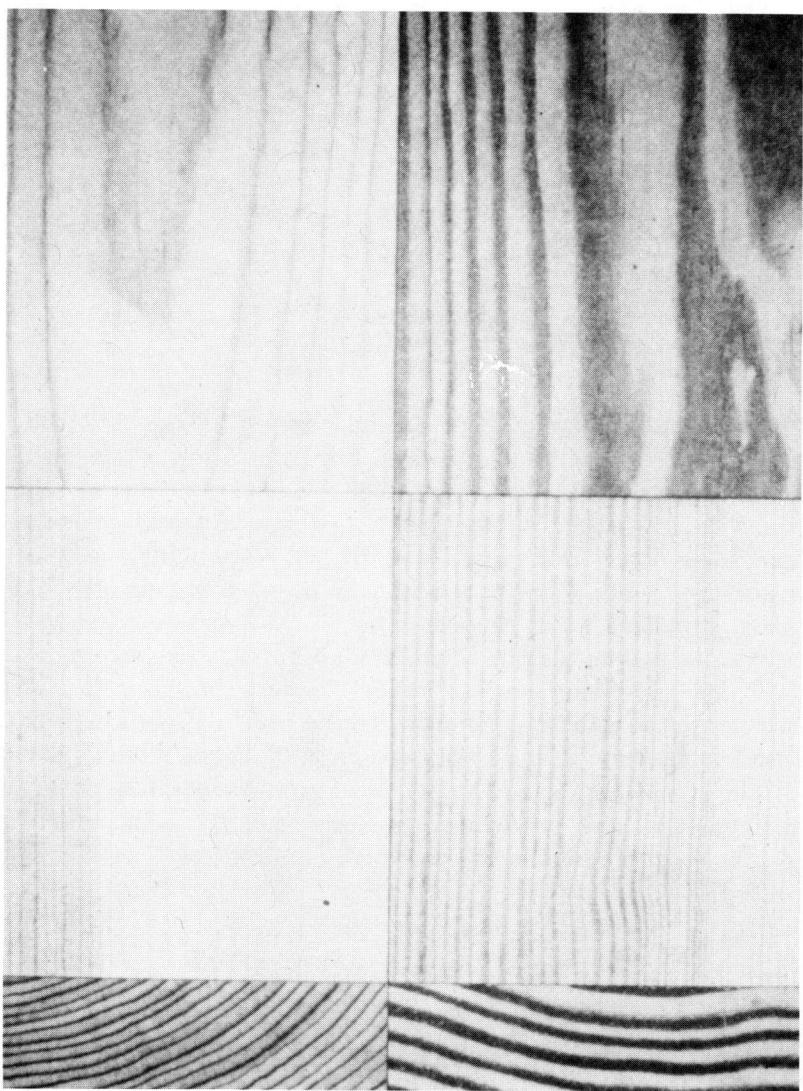

Figure 31. shortleaf pine

WALNUT   (Figure 32)

Walnut is a very hard, strong and heavy wood, quickly recognized by its rich chocolate to deep brown coloring which makes it unique among hardwoods. It has a mild distinctive odor when it is worked. Walnut has a fine uniform texture with a handsome interlocking grain pattern. It is very high in shock resistance. Walnut works easily with hand tools and machine tools, producing a very smooth finish.

Walnut is a dense wood and hard to burn. After burning and brushing the wood surface retains a dark brown color, and appears to be slightly rough due to the brushing, which reveals very small, narrow slits. The smallness of these slits is related to the denseness of the wood. Steel wool is not needed on a walnut surface as it is on other wood varieties, because of the denseness and hardness of this wood.

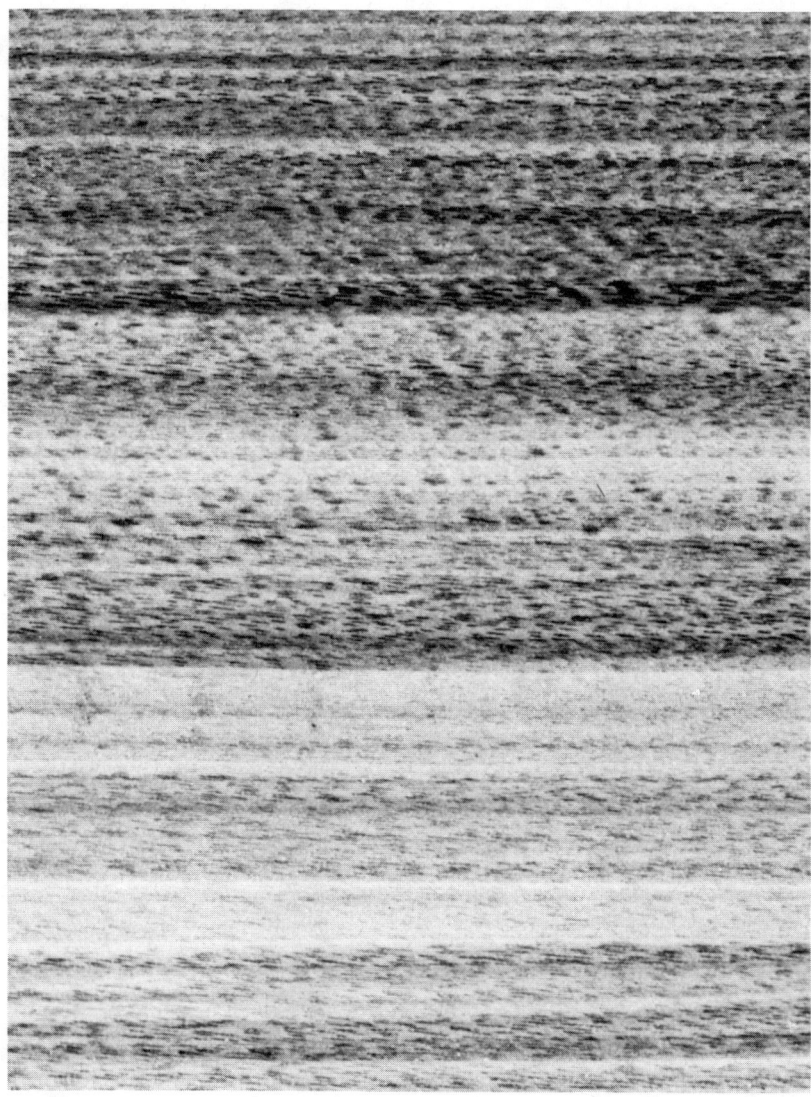

Figure 32. walnut

WHITE ASH   (Figure 33)

White ash ranges from brown to dark brown with a reddish tint. It is a hard strong stiff wood with very good shock resistance. It does however, have a tendency to split. It is very lustrous and works well with hand and machine tools. It remains smooth under continual rubbing.

White ash is a strong, dense hardwood and difficult to burn. It will require quite a lot of time to finish properly. After burning and brushing, the irregular grain pattern becomes quite noticeable and conspicuous ridging will result. This wood remains darkened by the burning process and does not regain any of the original wood color except in the bottom of the pithy areas after being brushed.

Figure 33. white ash

WHITE OAK   (Figure 34)

White oak is a very stiff wood ranging in color from a rich light brown to dark brown. White oak grain runs very straight. It is easily worked with hand and machine tools (except a shaper) and produces a very smooth finish.

It is similar in many qualities to red oak. It is a dense wood, and burns similarly to red oak, with ridges occurring after burning. After brushing with the steel brush, the springwood areas become pithy in appearance. The texture is rough in the pithy areas. This grain distinction could be developed into interesting patterns by using the pithy areas to form a design.

Figure 34. white oak

YELLOW POPLAR   (Figure 35)

Yellow poplar is light in weight, moderately stiff, and low in shock resistance. Poplar is difficult to work with hand and machine tools because it has a tendency to split and crack. It can be finished to a smooth surface and takes a high polish.

It burns fairly uniformly over the surface. After brushing, you will be able to detect ridging. The shallow areas are rough in texture, and brown in color while the other burnt surfaces are black.

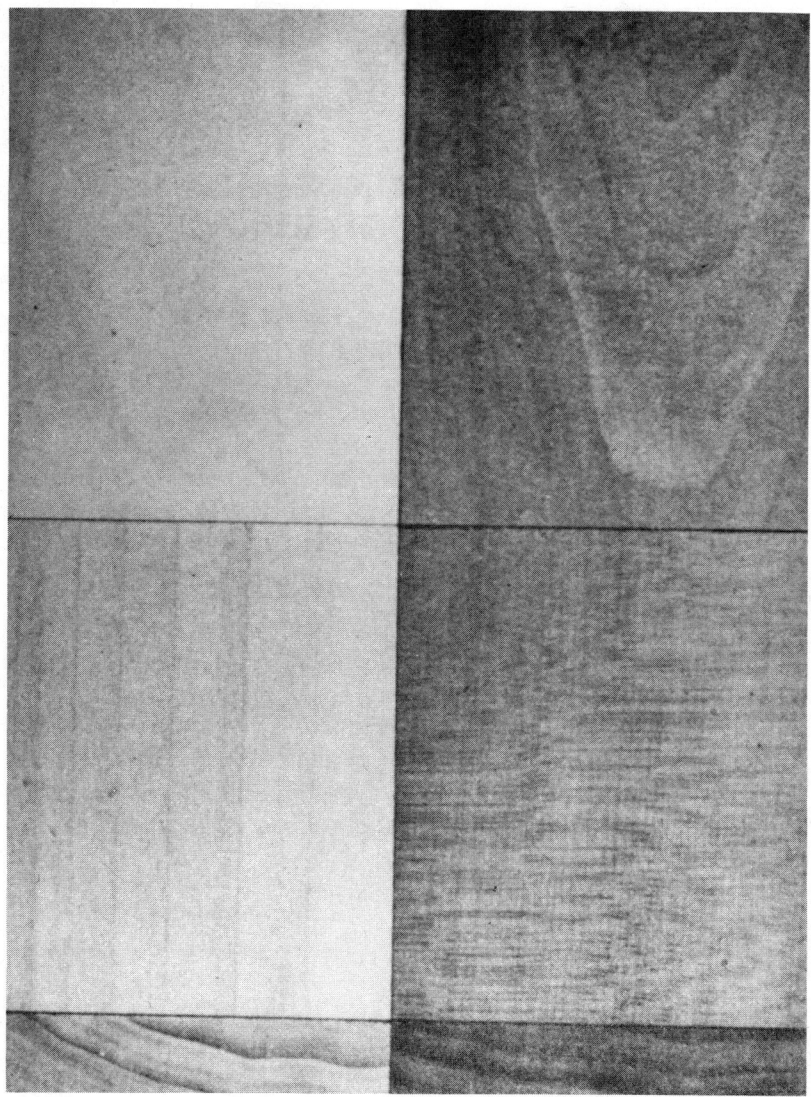

Figure 35. yellow poplar

LESS COMMON WOODS FOR USE IN WOOD BURNING

APPLE

Apple is dense and very hard and has a very fine grain. It is a pale reddish-brown in color and is easily worked with tools.

It does not char uniformly over the surface. Deep long narrow cracks develop in heavily charred areas. Ridges are not noticeable. Heavy charred regions do not have as smooth a surface or texture as areas which char only lightly. The areas which char lightly are of a medium brown color.

BLACK WILLOW

Black willow is a pale reddish-brown. It is lightweight and soft, but firm, with a very fine grain. It is also resistant to decay.

This wood chars very evenly forming no distinguishable ridges. After brushing some areas of the wood remain hard and smooth requiring little steel wooling. Surrounding areas require steel wool to achieve the smooth even surface that this fine textured wood can achieve.

BUCKEYE

This fine-grained wood is white to yellowish, soft, and lightweight. The grain is pronounced. It is difficult to work with and is not shock resistant nor is it resistant to decay.

This wood has a tendency to blister. No noticeable ridges form after burning. Brushing reveals low spots to the touch, but not to the eye. Its overall surface is very smooth after brushing. A very smooth dark brown color can be achieved with a finely textured surface.

CHESTNUT

This wood does not char uniformly. It forms distinct ridges which are more noticeable after brushing. The high ridges are much smoother than the lower areas which tend to be pithy in appearance. These ridges flow with the wood contour and are quite noticeable in appearance. The color stays primarily black or dark brown in a few spots. Steel wooling will not smooth the appearance of the lower ridges but their contrasting texture makes for an interesting effect.

COTTONWOOD

This wood is soft, lightweight and straight grained and is whitish to a yellowish-brown in color. The grain can be very pronounced. It resembles black willow. It is low in shock resistance and is not resistant to decay. It is also brittle and unstable and is difficult to work with tools.

Chars uniformly forming a smooth surface with no ridges and a uniform smooth brown color.

When brushed and steel wooled, the brown color of this wood becomes very uniform with no ridges appearing.

MAGNOLIA

This light colored wood has a very close-knit grain, with little difference in the color of the springwood and summerwood. It is moderately lightweight. It is smooth and is easy to work with tools. It is not very shock resistant and is not resistant to decay.

This wood chars very uniformly initially. Large cracks in the wood surface which enlarge and split with burning make the wood difficult to work with. No ridge forms on this wood after brushing. The grain is noticeable after burning. An even brown color along with a very smooth surface can be achieved after brushing and steel wooling. This is a very fine textured wood.

RED ALDER

The grain of the red alder resembles that of cherry and is popular for cabinet work. The wood is a pale reddish-brown, and is heavy. It is difficult to work with because of its brittle quality.

After burning, it develops small cracks running with the grain. Color changes to gray brown after brushing and steel wooling. Wide low ridges after brushing appear, and follow the contour of the grain.

SASSAFRAS

This wood is very hard to burn and requires a great deal of time if you decide to use it. After brushing, it forms ridges with the bottom of the ridge remaining the original color of the wood. Very little steel wooling is required because of the hardness of the wood. It forms a smooth finely textured surface when finished.

CORK

Cork can be purchased in sheets 2 feet by 3 feet and varies in thickness from 1/16 inch on up.

Cork deserves to be considered apart from the woods listed because it is a forest product but not truly a wood. It is the bark of several species of oak, mainly *Quercus suber*. Naturally when the bark is stripped from the tree, the tree dies.

If a pattern is being drawn on the cork, it may be necessary to go over the lead pencil lines with colored pencil or colored chalk. Lines drawn on the cork with lead pencil will not show well because of the texture and color of the cork.

Cork is used widely in wood burning because it is very lightweight and burns quickly, evenly, and easily. The electric pen is recommended, as the use of the torch would really serve no purpose. The electric pen is used with the pencil, needle, or blade point depending on how wide and deep the line is to be.

Crayon, tempera paints, felt tip pen, and acrylic artist paints are all recommended for finishing the burned area

ART OF WOOD BURNING

only. In addition if you want the burned area to darken, use a brush and apply lemon oil or peanut oil.

PRESSED BOARD

Pressed board, which is basically left-over or scrap wood chips glued together can be used for certain wood burning projects. It has an interesting design and color composition and with care, can be burned smoothly despite the ups and downs the electric pen must take. Its main advantage over the other materials is that is is much cheaper than other woods. The blade point makes a very fine line while the pencil point can be used to make a wider burned area. The object can then be decorated with color leaf foil or by burning crayon on the lines. If you burn the design deeply and widely enough you can also paint the unburned parts. Sanding should not be necessary with pressed board.

PLYWOOD

Plywood, which is thin layers of pine pressed together, may have a layer of cherry or other wood on the top. It is considered excellent for burning. It is inexpensive in price and has a pronounced grain as well as an interesting color pattern. When burned, it forms deep ridges and the different colors of the wood are still noticeable after burning. Many lumber stores have scrap pieces of plywood for sale, so you don't necessarily have to buy a 4 foot by 8 foot sheet. The thickness you buy will depend on the requirements of the project.

CHAPTER 4

Template Making

Templates, or patterns as they are often called, are used in wood burning to reproduce the same pattern or design repeatedly on a wood or cork surface. Templates if used correctly can be utilized over and over again without destroying them. When referring to templates we speak in terms of *negative* and *positive* design templates.

In negative design the flame is used to make the design along the outer border of the metal template, leaving the actual pattern the natural wood color (Figure 36).

In positive design the pattern is burned and is surrounded by the natural wood (Figure 36).

As with all crafts, the design ideas you develop will identify and compliment you, the originator. Take time to choose and develop your design. Consider wood burning and its capabilities as well as the material you are burning. Start with simple designs and as you grow more at ease with wood burning try more intricate patterns. Ideas are everywhere. Just look around. Combining simple ideas into more intricate ones can produce unusual and exciting visual patterns.

MAKING YOUR TEMPLATE

Sheet metal lies flat on the wood surface and comes in various widths, lengths and thicknesses. Eighteen gauge sheet metal is recommended because it can be cut easily with the recommended tin snips. Unless your sheet metal is thick enough, a torch will warp the metal and curl it, causing the wood underneath to burn. Avoid galvanized metal. Flattened

tin cans will not be adequate because they heat quickly and the burning will not leave clearly defined lines. The tools for template making are:
- (1) tin snips
- (2) ⅜" cold chisel
- (3) ball peen hammer
- (4) jewelers saw
- (5) scratch awl
- (6) small files
- (7) leather work gloves

Buy a piece of sheet metal of convenient size. Select a piece that is larger than your pattern to allow for scrap or design changes. If you are doing a positive design template, allow 1½ inches margin on each side of the template, from the edge of the pattern to the edge of the piece of sheet metal. Too much scrap or margin will become a waste and a problem when trying to use the jewelers saw.

Use your scratch awl as you would use a pencil to mark off the piece of sheel metal you want to start with. Start to cut the sheet metal with the tin snips along the marked line. When you get to the point where you cannot cut any further with the tin snips because of the length of the snips blade, use your cold chisel and hammer to cut the rest of the way by placing the chisel on the cutting line and striking the chisel with the hammer. A good pair of leather work gloves will help protect your hands from the sharp metal edges.

For the beginner:

Try using a good sized cookie cutter as a pattern to trace onto your sheet metal to make your first template. Cookie cutters are easy to trace and make a good starting project.

If you are cutting a positive design template use the following procedure:

- (1) use the scratch awl to trace your design onto the sheet metal

ART OF WOOD BURNING 69

Figure 36. Here are examples of both negative and positive templates.

Upper right—a positive pattern of natural wood surrounded by burned area.

Upper left—a negative or burned design.

Lower left—a positive template.

Lower right—a negative template from which the positive template was made.

(2) drive a nail all the way through a section of metal that will be cut away and discarded
(3) loosen one end of the blade from the jewelers saw frame to free it
(4) place the loose end of the blade through the nail hole.
(5) fasten the loose end of the blade back into the jewelers saw frame and tighten up the blade
(6) clamp, or hold, the piece of sheet metal down firmly to the work table so the metal doesn't bend or twist
(7) saw along the pattern lines with the jewelers saw
(8) after you have finished cutting remove the saw by loosening one end of the blade from the frame and slipping the sheet metal over the loose end

If you are cutting a negative design template you need to use the following procedure:
(1) trace the pattern
(2) clamp to a work table or hold the metal tightly to prevent twisting and bending
(3) use the tin snips, hammer, chisel, and the jewelers saw to cut the pattern along the borders

Curves, angles, and strips are easily cut by proper use of the proper tools (Figure 37).

After you have finished cutting the pattern, place the pattern on a flat working surface and use your hammer to pound the template, (particularly the edges), so that it will lay perfectly flat on the wood surface. You may want to file the jagged edges of your template to smooth them so they will not scratch the wood surface.

Flame is then applied to the patterned edge of the template. The template is moved backward to burn each new area. By moving the template backward the burned area can be kept parallel.

Avoid sharp angles and thin sections.

Figure 37. Edge patterns that can be used in a series to create a repetitive design.

CHAPTER 5

Projects

Wood burning has unlimited potential and may be used to create many useful household items. Projects for the kitchen include candle holders, salad bowls, wooden canisters, wooden bread boxes, bread and cheese boards, salt and pepper shakers, trays, and napkin holders.

Many attractive prefinished items are sold in hobby stores that are meant for decoupage but they can be wood burned as well. These items come in a variety of woods including cherry, mahogany, white pine, basswood, pressed board, and plywood. Some items will be a mixture of woods, that is the sides will be made of plywood and the bottom of basswood. As long as the area you intend to burn is all of one wood, this mixture will not interfere, since the two types of woods will burn differently and at different rates. But if this difference is to be part of your pattern, these items will still not present a problem to you.

Prefinished items include wooden purses, jewelry boxes of every shape including the treasure chest type, bread boards, salt and pepper shakers, picture and mirror frames, wall plaques, candle holders, what-not-shelves, vanity trays, pencil caddies, calendar and address files, and trays. These items after burning will require little sanding since they are prefinished. In some cases, such as recipe files and kleenex box holders, the wood can sometimes be very thin. So be careful not to burn too deeply.

There is really no end to the projects that you can decorate with wood burning, including the front edges of book shelves that are installed on tracks and brackets on walls.

There are even special wood burning kits available with patterns already stenciled on the wood for you and are ready to assembly and burn. These include recipe racks, hanging utensil racks for the kitchen, bird houses, storage boxes, and desk organizers.

Projects can be made using the torch or pencil or a combination of both. Both methods are versatile and can be adapted to any project you may wish to make. For a beginner torch project we have selected a tray to give you some directions regarding procedure and precautions we think are necessary.

TORCH PROJECTS
Burning Your Own Tray

This project is excellent for the beginner in the wood burning craft. It allows for individual creativity in the design of each tray. You will need:
(1) propane torch
(2) pine slab, 2 inches or more in thickness. Softwoods like pine are easier and require less time than hardwoods. However, almost any wood can be used.
(3) small steel brush
(4) asbestos glove and pad
(5) peanut oil or wax

Take your piece of wood and cut it to ½ inch larger in length and width than the final size you want. The extra wood allows for loss in shaping.

The shape of the sides of your tray can be formed in several ways. One way is with a circular saw. Another way is to "burn" and design your shape into the sides of your tray through burning and brushing. This method would be an interesting and creative way to shape the sides.

First, with pencil outline the shape of the burned out area you plan to have in the finished project. Then light your propane torch and burn lightly over the area you have marked (Figure 38A). Do not hold the torch in one place for a long period of

ART OF WOOD BURNING 75

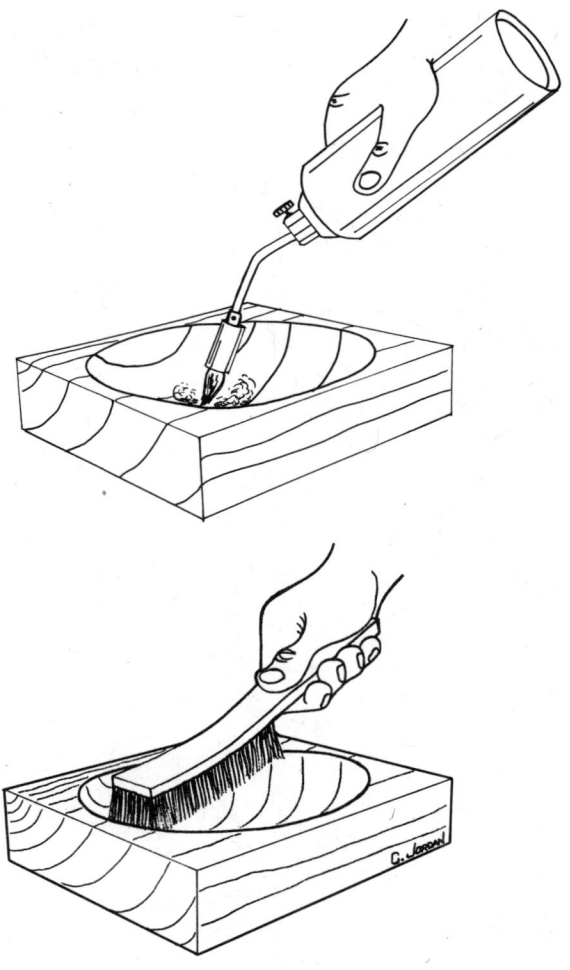

Figure 38. A—Upper left—Use the propane torch to burn the inside to the desired depth.
B—Lower left—Use the steel brush to brush the burned area.

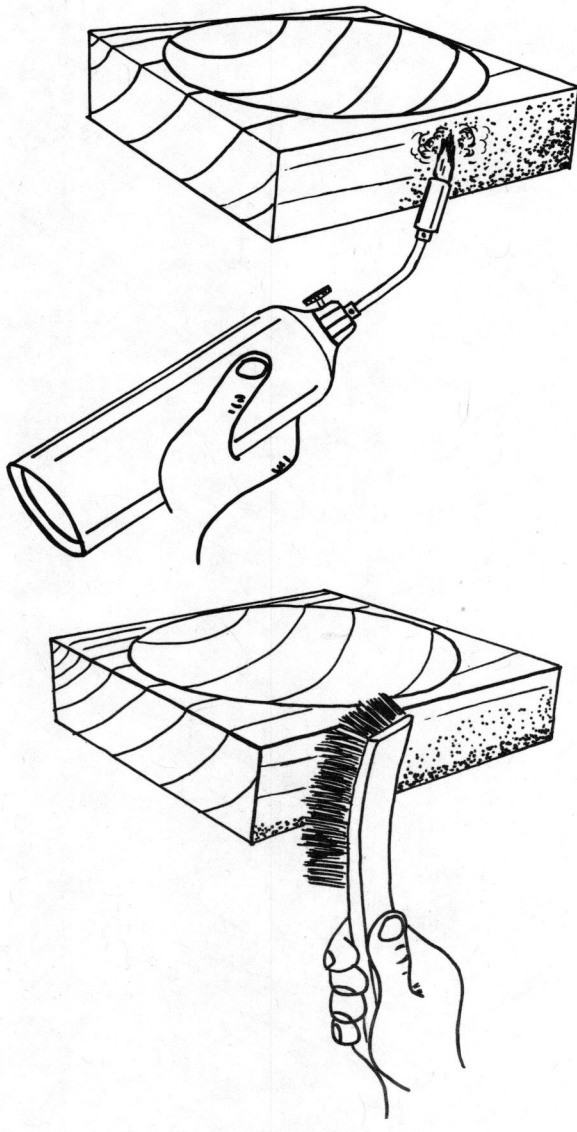

C—Upper center—Burn the sides of the tray with the torch.
D—Lower center—Brush the burned sides with the steel brush.

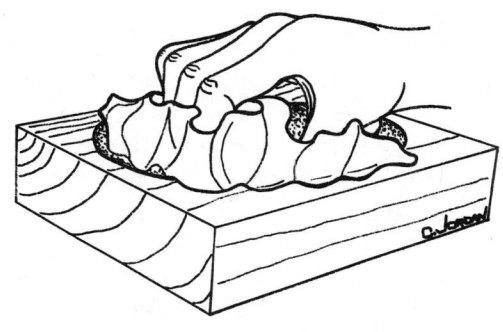

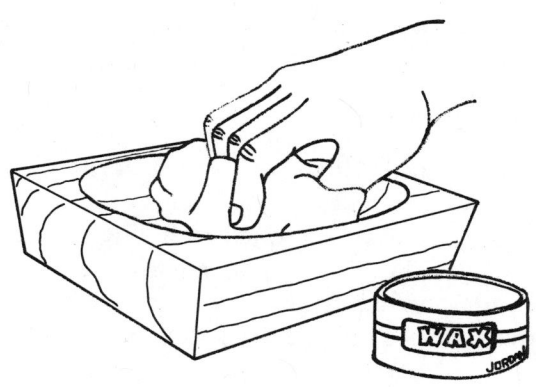

E—Upper right—Use the steel wool to smooth the inside and sides of the tray.

F—Lower right—Rub the finished tray with peanut oil or wax.

time hoping to speed up the process of burning. By doing this, you will only disintegrate the wood, create a fire hazard, and ruin the project. Take your steel brush and brush the burned surface of your wood to loosen and remove the burned wood (Figure 38B). Brush *with* the grain along the piece of wood. *Do not* brush across the grain, since it will scratch and mar the surface.

Continue burning and brushing until you reach the desired depth for your tray. The sloping sides will require less burning and brushing.

Finish the sides and bottom of your tray by lightly burning and brushing to the desired shape (Figure 38C, 38D). After you have finished with the torch and achieved the desired depth smooth the surface with very fine sandpaper and finish with no. 000 steel wool (Figure 38E).

To finish the tray, rub peanut oil or wax into the wood (Figure 38F). This will darken the blacked areas and bring out the dark brown areas to a richer brown color.

A fine example to a finished tray is shown here, the work of Barbara Davey of Raleigh, North Carolina (Figure 39).

Furniture

Application of pencil designs or torch to furniture, old or new, will create a unique appearance. Use of the pencil to burn designs into the surface or the torch to lightly scorch the surface are not new ideas. Furniture must be wood and must not be plastic. The torch method is known as the "blow torch method." It is used mainly on softwood such as pine, fir and cypress to create a rustic or antiqued effect. To achieve the effect you need only slightly scorch the surface of the furniture with the propane torch. The resin in the softwood generally keeps these woods from burning quickly. Furnitures made of hardwoods or other varieties can be done by the same method, but due to darkness of some varieties of hardwoods, the scorched effect may not be as visible. The blow torch is generally used in new furniture on which no finish has been applied. If you decide to

ART OF WOOD BURNING

try this method we urge you to be *cautious*. Allow adequate ventilation for smoke and if possible do it outside on a windless day. Keep a fire extinguisher nearby or fireproof blanket to smother the flames if the furniture catches fire.

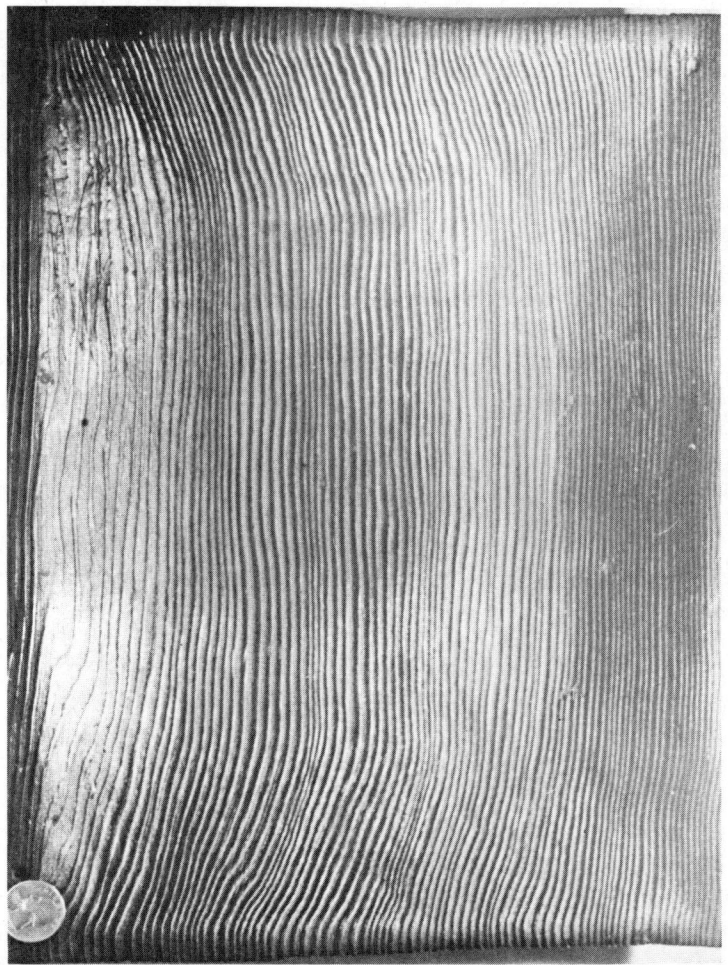

Figure 39. A tray made by torching, showing wood grain.

Pencil & Stencil

Templates are not restricted for use with torches. They make ideal stencils to trace around using the wood burning pencil. If you find difficulty in using the electric pencil (Figure 8) try using your template to guide you in the use of this new tool. Later, when your hand has become accustomed to drawing curves, angles, and straight lines with the pen, you may try some freehand design using no template.

Also available are metal alphabet and branding sets with different patterns, which can be used as templates. They fit over the tip of the pen and when heated evenly are just placed on the wood until the pattern in dark enough.

Many templates that are used with the torches may also be used with the pen. Use an asbestos glove to hold the template down while you are using the pen to burn around the pattern.

For drawing straight lines, use a piece of scrap metal with a straight edge, so you can burn along the edge of the metal very smoothly. The blade overpoint is probably best for this type of work.

Chessboard

A very beautiful and interesting project for the advanced wood burner would be the chessboard. For this project you will need:

(1) 18" by 18" by ½" thick piece of wood preferably cherry, maple, or plywood with a cherry or maple surface
(2) ruler and pencil
(3) wood burning pencil with blade, needle, and hole cutting points
(4) finishing supplies—oil, sand paper, wax, etc.

If you are using a solid piece of wood instead of plywood, you must cut the wood into strips and reglue it together to prevent warping. If you do not have access to a wood working shop, inquire at the local hobby shop for sections of wood that have been cut into strips and reglued. Most of the solid wood used as

Figure 40. This salt shaker is of white pine.

plaques, boxes, book ends, etc. has been cut and reglued. If you are using plywood, you do not need to cut and reglue your wood. It is ready to use.

After you have obtained your wood, measure off 1½ inches around the entire piece for the border. Measure off the squares for the chessboard pattern allowing 1 inch for each one. Mark all the lines lightly in pencil. Pencil in the design you want for the border. Allow your electric pencil to heat up for several minutes. Burn your design into the surface using a sheet of sheet metal with a straight edge to make the straight lines even. After you have completed all burning you may then apply any decoration or finish as described in Chapter 6.

Monogramming

Monogramming can be done either with the electric pen or with the torch. If you are using the torch, you will need to make a template for the letters; either a positive or negative template, depending on whether you want the letter to be burned in, or outlined in the surrounding wood burned area.

If you are using the electric pen to monogram you can use either of the templates to guide your pen around. As mentioned earlier some hobby craft companies have monogramming kits available for use with electric pens. In addition you may wish to draw your initials in the material with a pencil and use the pen to burn along the lines. Monogramming is particularly good for coasters, hot pads, and bread and cheese trays.

Wall Plaques

If you would like to start from scratch, you can cut and shape the edges of the wood for your plaque. However, many hobby stores have a large variety of different shapes and sizes of wall plaques you can choose from. The edges will be turned and shaped much more delicately than you will be able to do by hand. They come in every shape and style imagineable from the elegant to the rustic. They are made of different types of -wood Basswood and white pine are the most common. But

ART OF WOOD BURNING 83

avoid any that are pre-stained because during the burning, you could scratch or damage the stain, and would have a difficult time touching up the damaged area.

Figure 41. This wall plaque is of Honduras mahogany.

You will see some wall plaques that appear to consist of strips of wood. The wood has been cut into strips and reglued to keep the wood from warping. These will require more skill to burn evenly where the glue is present.

Trace your pattern onto the wall plaque. Then use the electric pen to burn in the design, choosing the point that will make a deep and wide enough line for you. Finish the plaque to suit your individual taste. Place a picture hook on the back and it is ready to hang up and display.

Picture and Mirror Frames

Picture and mirror frames present a challenge because the area to be burned is usually narrow and is sometimes irregular in shape. Repetitive designs with curves and lines are ideal for such small areas. You can either trace the design from a book and draw it on the frame using the standard procedure or you may use a template with repetitive designs that you have already made. The electric pen is recommended since the torch is meant to use on larger areas.

Coasters

Plastic coasters may be bought that are lined with cork and can be decorated with wood burning. Choose a design that is small enough to fit on the cork. Trace your design on the cork using the standard procedure. If the design shows too faintly, go over it with a colored pencil. Then use your electric pen with the needle or pencil point and burn in the design. The burned design may then be painted if desired.

Coasters that are completely wood can also be wood burned. Using the pencil or needle point burn some repetitive lines or curves into the upper rim of the coaster. Then burn your design on the inside bottom of the coaster. Both foil and crayon are recommended for decorating. Then cover the inside and top edge of the coaster with clear lacquer to make the design and color waterproof. Paints and felt tip pencils are also recommended for decorating the burned area.

Foil Art

Special colored leaf foil is sold by hobby stores for use in wood burning and is used mainly for the purpose of decorating. It comes in colors as well as gold and silver. The gold and silver will not be reflected as well if the object to be burned is in a vertical position, such as a tray or coaster. The needle point is usually used, or if a wider line is required, the blade point may be used.

Select a design from the book or select your own original design and draw it on a sheet of tracing paper. Then place the foil with the colored side up, under the tracing. Place over the item to be burned. Then steadily but firmly, using the selected point, carefully trace the design without lifting the pen. Lifting will break the design. Be sure the foil does not slip around, as this will cause an uneven pattern.

This same technique can be used for cork as well as leather. If you should want to be sure that abrasion or wear does not rub off the foil color, it can be finished with lacquer.

Colored Wood Burning With Crayon

This unusually attractive colored wood burning can be made on a range of wooden objects from plaques to trays.

Trace your design onto a sheet of tracing paper. Then take a crayon and go over the lines of the drawing. Place the drawing, with the crayon side down on the object. Use the electric pen with the needle or pencil point to go over the drawing.

If your design includes a large area that requires crayon, such as a cluster of grapes, or a red apple, the following procedure is recommended. After you trace the design on the tracing paper, use the crayon to color in the area, such as the green leaves or the grapes. Then place the traced design with the crayon-side down on the wood and place an iron that has been heated to medium over the complete design. Leave the iron in place for several seconds. Then life the iron and paper from the wood.

For making freehand type lines, curves, and patterns the following method is recommended. Take a piece of aluminum foil and using a crayon of the desired color, smear a smooth layer of crayon on the less shiny side of the foil. Place the foil on the wood, crayon-side down. Etch the designs on the shiny side of the foil with the electric pen and then display the results.

Crayon can also be used as a method of coloring your burned design. Take the crayon and carefully smear a smooth layer of crayon over the burned area. Take the electric pen and burn evenly over the crayon so that it melts into the wood. Be careful that you do not smudge the edges of the design. Darker colored crayons do a better job at covering the burned areas than do the light colors such as yellow.

The crayon can then be covered with a layer of lacquer to keep it from wearing or rubbing off.

CORK PROJECTS

Place Mats

Cut your place mats from a sheet of cork with a pair of scissors. 1/16 or 1/8 inch thickness is best. Trace your design from the book onto the cork using the standard procedure. Then, using the electric pen with the pencil, needle, or blade point, burn the design into the cork. Do not burn so deeply that you burn through the cork. The burned area can then be decorated by burning crayon in it, felt tip pen, acrylic, or tempera paints. Peanut or lemon oil may also be brushed in if you merely want to darken the burned area.

You can buy cork place mats that already have the design stenciled on and are ready for burning. Some very beautiful designs including Pennsylvania Dutch are available. Either way, you can have 4 beautiful hand decorated cork place mats for less than $2.00.

Bulletin Board

You will need a ½ inch thick piece of cork cut to size and

enough prestained ½ or ¾ inch wide molding to cover the edges of the cork. Cut the molding to the lengths needed to cover the 4 edges, cutting the corners at 45° angles so they will fit together and form right angles. Then use finishing nails to nail the molding in place around the edges of the cork.

Trace your design onto the cork. Using the electric pen with the pencil, needle or blade point, burn your design into the cork. Decorate your burned design with crayon, felt tip pen, acrylic paint or tempera paints if desired. Then attach a picture hanger or pieces of special adhesive sold for use with mirrors and bulletin boards.

Hot Pads

Hot pads are a project well suited to cork. The ½ inch thick cork is recommended as it will absorb more heat. Cut your piece of cork from the sheet with a pair of scissors. Then trace your design onto the cork using the standard procedure. Use the pencil, needle, or blade point to burn your design in with the electric pen. If desired the burned area can then be decorated by using crayon, felt tip pen, acrylic artist paint, or tempera. All of these hold up well under heat and will not be harmed by continued use.

CHAPTER 6

Finishes

The final job is the finish. You can bring out the beauty of the grain of your wood with this procedure, and, if you wish, cahnge the color of the wood with a stain.

We will indicate two finishing methods and a decorative method at the end of this chapter. The one you use will depend upon how and where the project will be used, the type of wood from which it is made and the final appearance desired.

If your project is to remain in an area that is humid, such as a basement, or if you live in a section of the country where humidity levels vary greatly we recommend that you follow Finishing Method #1. This finish uses a sealer which minimizes moisture loss or gain. Wood can absorb humidity from the air. High humidity levels can cause wood to swell. Similarly low humidity levels can cause wood to shrink due to loss of water. This swelling and shrinking can result in the wood cracking and splitting if it is not well sealed.

If an object is to be used outdoors, you will need to use a marine paint on the unburned parts as the finishing layer to seal out the water and delay decay.

Finishing Method #2 will not prevent shrinking and swelling because it does not seal the pores of the wood.

All woods will not react in the same manner to the same finish. Finishing Method #2, described further on does not provide a high glossy finish for all woods. The best way to determine if it will produce a high polish on your wood is to use a test piece of the same wood as your project. Apply the finish, polish, and determine for yourself whether the result is to your taste.

The finished appearance will depend upon the finishing method used; in particular, staining. With the use of stains, you can change the color of the wood, darken the original color, or leave the wood in its natural state. You can use stains to make some types of wood resemble other woods. For instance, you can stain butternut to resemble walnut and pine to resemble maple.

Water colors can be used to paint in certain areas of your burned design. If you intend to use water colors they must be used *before* the filler coat is applied or they will not absorb into the wood. You can only use Finishing Method #1 if you decide to use water colors. The use of linseed oil in Finishing Method #2 will cause water colors to bleed out of the wood and become smeared.

Before you apply any finish to your project you must prepare the wood for the finish. After you have completed burning and brushing your project to the desired shape and size you will notice that some areas of the surface or the entire surface still may feel rough. Use a very fine sand paper, (No. 220), or even finer, (No. 600), to lightly sand these rough areas smooth. Remember to sand with the grain and be careful; some varieties of softwood, such as pine, do not take sanding and you may sand away the effects your burning has created. After you have smoothed the surface with the sand paper, use a tack cloth to remove all possible dirt. Tack cloth is a lint free soft cloth, such as an old handkerchief. Dampen the tack cloth with water, and a few drops of turpentine and varnish, in order to pick up all the surface dirt.

As your next step, lightly brush the surface with No. 000 steel wool to smooth the surface once more. After you have finished go back over the entire surface and check with the fingertips for any rough places that you might have missed and remove all bits of steel wool that may be left on the surface.

Now you are ready to begin applying the finish. We will discuss two methods of finishing, which are adequate for the beginner, yet challenging enough for the more advanced wood craftsman.

ART OF WOOD BURNING

Steps—Finishing Method #1; For humid areas, basements, areas with sharp changes in humidity.
1. Sand
2. Dust
3. Stain (optional)
4. Steel wool
5. Filler coat
6. Glaze
7. Sealer
8. Gloss coat (lacquer, varnish, shellac or wax)

Staining: An optional part of wood finishing, which may be used to change the shade or tone of the wood surface. Stain is brushed on to insure even application, then wiped off while still wet, with a lint free cloth. Remember, brush and wipe with the grain and not across it.

Filler: A transparent liquid that is brushed on with a paint brush. It is brushed with the grain and then across the grain to seal all pores in the wood surface. When the pores are filled the surface will become hard and smooth after drying.

Glaze: A transparent liquid that is brushed on over the filler coat. It produces a shaded, antiqued effect over the surface.

Sealer: A transparent liquid that is brushed on. It seals the entire surface and prepares the wood for the final gloss coat. Before you apply the final gloss coat, *lightly* sand the surface with No. 220 sand paper.

The *gloss* coat is the final coat. It is brushed or sprayed on. You may choose a lacquer finish, a varnish finish, or a shellac finish. All coats are brushed on over the entire surface, front and back, and each coat should be dry before applying the next. Shellac will darken as it ages and should be avoided if darkening will be unattractive.

Steps—Finishing Method #2
1. Sand
2. Dust
3. Steel wool
4. Linseed oil

5. Paste wax

This second method of finishing a project does not seal the pores of the wood. It involves the use of linseed oil and floor paste wax. Linseed oil is brushed uniformly over the entire surface and the excess oil removed with a lint free cloth. Go with the grain in both steps. Uneven application of oil will cause spots to appear where excess oil has soaked in. Allow oil to dry for 48 hours, then use a lint free cloth to rub paste wax evenly into the wood surface. Allow the wax to dry, then buff by hand. It may take several applications of waxing and buffing to achieve a high gloss depending on the type of wood. Other types of oil such as peanut oil may be substituted for linseed oil for projects that will be used in connection with food.

Decorative Methods

Several methods of decoration can be used with wood burning patterns. Foil, crayon, paint and felt tip pen are used to decorate your project with color. Paints are used not only for wood burning but also for cork burned designs. Color can be applied with a brush when using paints. The electric pencil is necessary to apply the crayon and colored foil.

The entire surface of a plaque or object can be painted, taking care not to cover the wood burned design. If the design is covered slightly, simply go over the design with the electric pencil. In addition, felt tip pens can be used to decorate the burned area as can acrylic artist paint and tempera.

On all projects in which some manner of decoration is present such as foil, crayon or paint, you need to be especially careful in applying your finish. We recommend using a test piece with a sample of the paint, foil or crayon you are using. Lemon oil with beeswax, a mineral oil base, generally sold for decoupage is quite suitable for crayon and paint decoration but not for foil.

Varnish or shellac can also be used over decoration. Again we recommend using a test piece with a sample of the crayon, foil, or paint that you are using. Apply the coat of shellac or varnish lightly with a fine brush. Do not brush the surface heavily. Shellac and varnish do not need two applications of sealer and filler coat like lacquer, but they are recommended nonetheless. However, if the filler and sealer coats are causing smearing you can leave them out and just apply the varnish or shellac. After each coat is applied, allow it to dry and apply the next coat until you have achieved a high gloss finish.

Whether as a hobby or for profit, we hope that this ancient woodcrafting technique provides hours of fun and relaxation together with pride in your finished projects.

PATTERNS FOR WOOD BURNING
Figures – Human and Animal

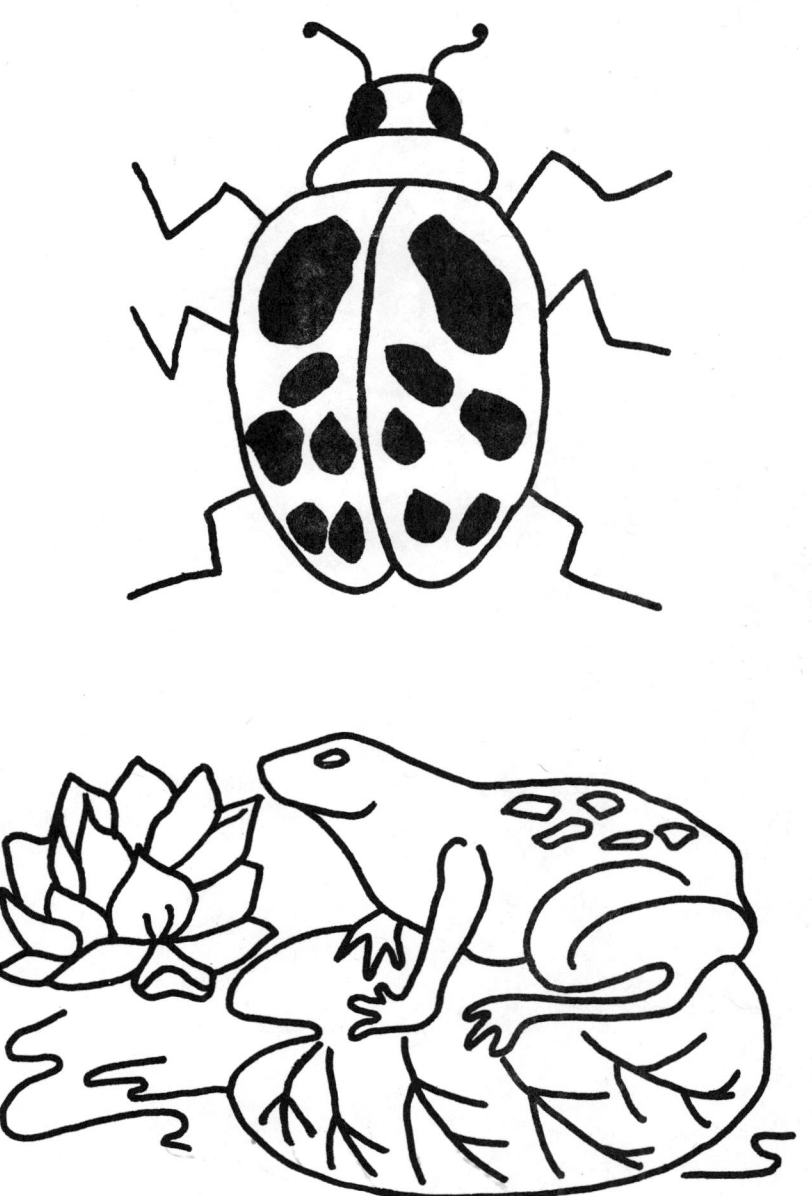

Plants, Flowers and Vegetables

Common Objects

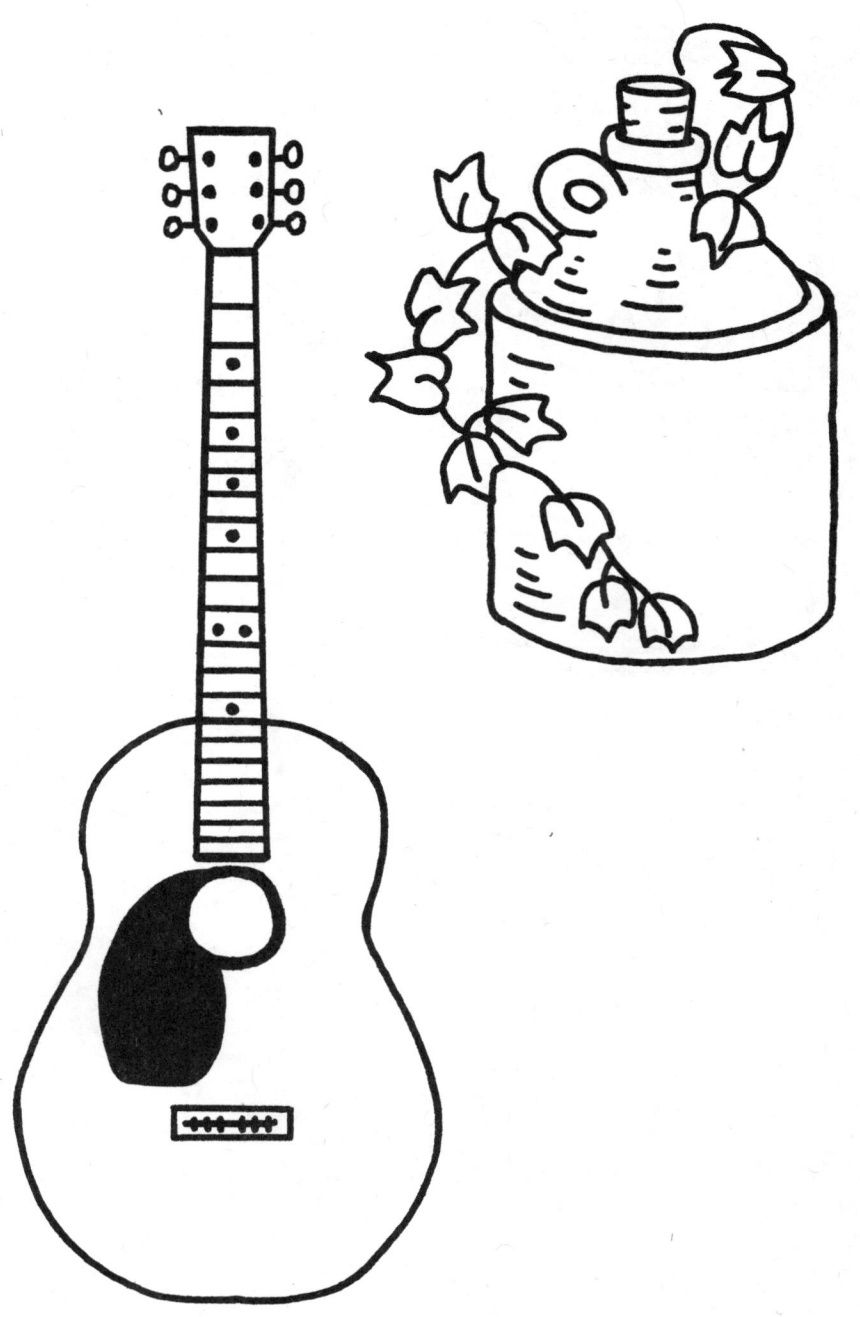

Abstractions

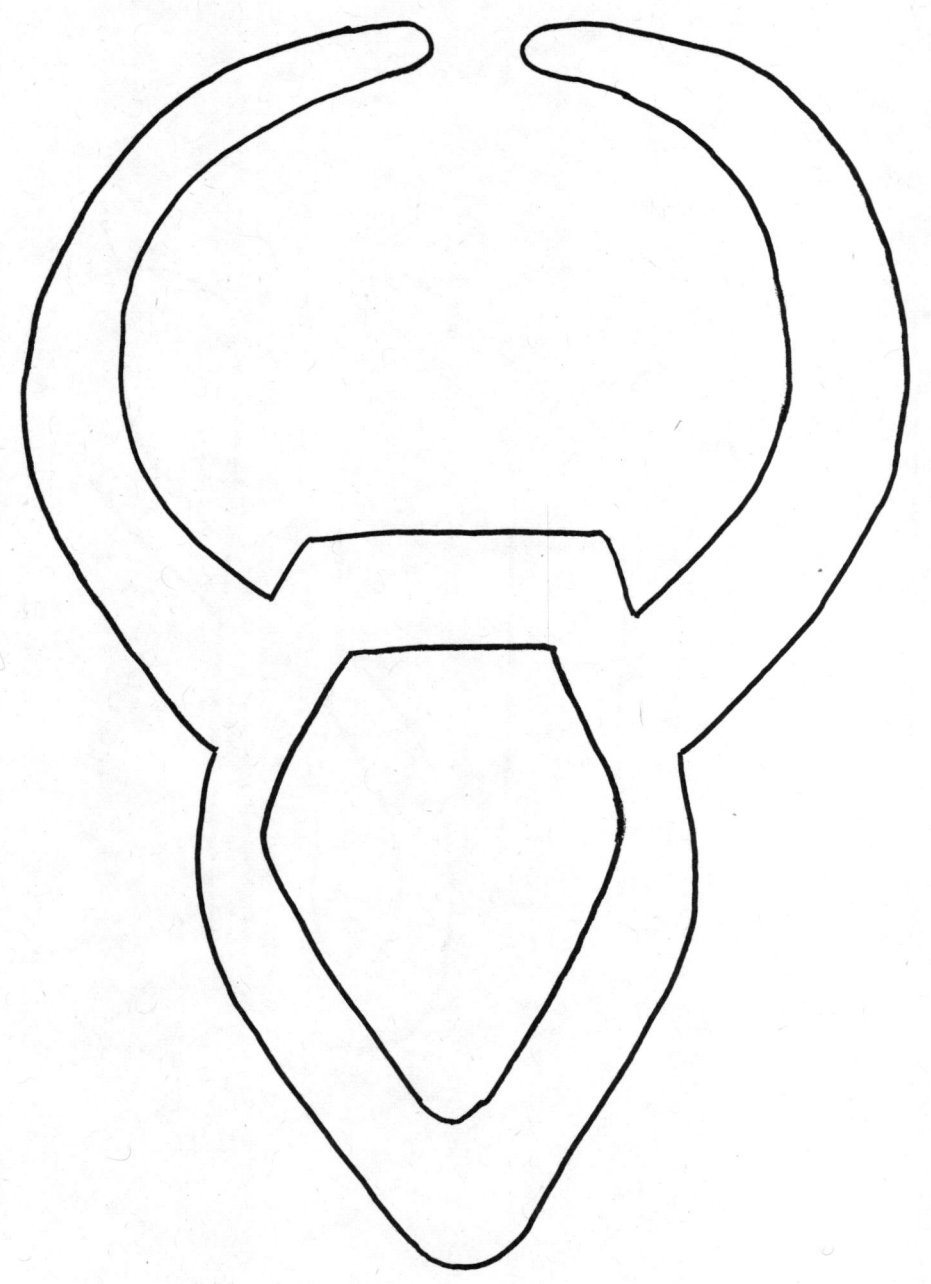